T0039925

EASY JAZZ FAVORITES

15 Selections For Young Jazz Ensembles

Contents

HAL•LEONARD®
CORPORATION
7777 W. BLUEMOUND RD. P.O. BOX 13819 MILWAUKEE, WI 53213

AIN'T MISBEHAVIN'

Trumpet 2

Words by ANDY RAZAF
Music by THOMAS WALLER and HARRY BROOKS
Arranged by BOB LOWDEN

ALL THE THINGS YOU ARE
(From VERY WARM FOR MAY)

TRUMPET 2

Lyrics by OSCAR HAMMERSTEIN II
Music by JEROME KERN
Arranged by MICHAEL SWEENEY

TRUMPET 2

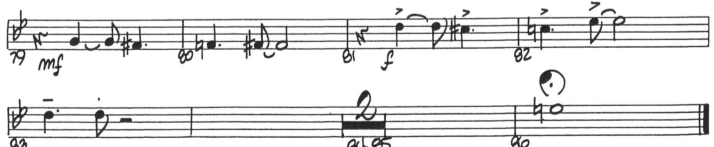

BLUE TRAIN
(Blue Trane)

TRUMPET 2

MODERATE SWING (♫ = ♩♪)

By JOHN COLTRANE
Arranged by MICHAEL SWEENEY

TRUMPET 2

CARAVAN
(From SOPHISTICATED LADIES)

Words and Music by DUKE ELLINGTON,
IRVING MILLS and JUAN TIZOL
Arranged by MICHAEL SWEENEY

TRUMPET 2

CHAMELEON

TRUMPET 2

**By HERBIE HANCOCK, PAUL JACKSON,
HARVEY MASON and BENNIE MAUPIN**
Arranged by MICHAEL SWEENEY

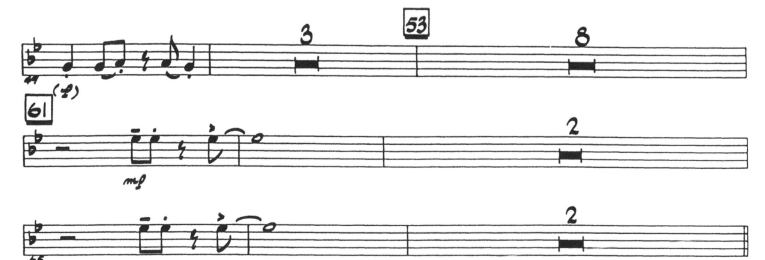

D.S. AL CODA

FLY ME TO THE MOON
(In Other Words)

Trumpet 2

Words and Music by BART HOWARD
Arranged by JERRY NOWAK

TRUMPET 2

THE GIRL FROM IPANEMA
(Garôta De Ipanema)

TRUMPET 2

Original Words by VINICIUS DE MORAES
Music by ANTONIO CARLOS JOBIM
Arranged by JOHN BERRY

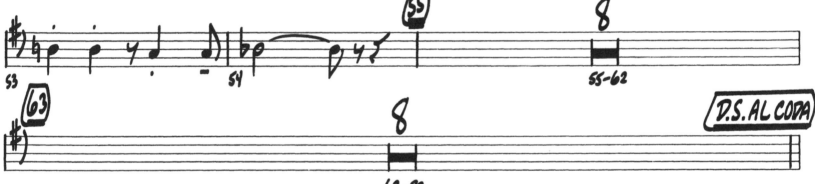

IN THE MOOD

TRUMPET 2

By JOE GARLAND
Arranged by MICHAEL SWEENEY

INSIDE OUT

TRUMPET 2

By MICHAEL SWEENEY

TRUMPET 2

MILESTONES

TRUMPET 2

By MILES DAVIS
Arranged by PETER BLAIR

TRUMPET 2

D.S. AL CODA
(W/REPEAT)

CODA

A NIGHTINGALE SANG
IN BERKELEY SQUARE

Lyric by ERIC MASCHWITZ
Music by MANNING SHERWIN
Arranged by ROGER HOLMES

Trumpet 2

ONE NOTE SAMBA
(Samba De Uma Nota So)

Original Lyrics by NEWTON MENDONCA
English Lyrics by ANTONIO CARLOS JOBIM
Music by ANTONIO CARLOS JOBIM
Arranged by JERRY NOWAK

TRUMPET 2

08060016

MCA music publishing

TRUMPET 2

080500016 P.2

ROUTE 66

TRUMPET 2

By BOBBY TROUP
Arranged by MICHAEL SWEENEY

TRUMPET 2

ST. LOUIS BLUES

TRUMPET 2

Words and Music by W.C. HANDY
Arranged by MICHAEL SWEENEY

WHEN I FALL IN LOVE

Words by EDWARD HEYMAN
Music by VICTOR YOUNG
Arranged by ROGER HOLMES

TRUMPET 2

TRUMPET 2